B

now you can

LIVE FREE!

Ten Modern MYTHS that shackle us without lawful basis are herein—BUSTED!

"There are none so enslaved as those who falsely believe they are free."

Goethe

How to live totally free from "the system" set up by the governments, courts and banks to steal your money and/or jail you.

How to eliminate all lawsuits, traffic tickets, debts, etc. and much, much more.

TRUE FREEDOM IS REALLY *FUN!*

By Bob Plimpton

0-9767181-0-3

LCCN 2005922918

Printed in the United States of America

Dedication

This book is dedicated to our
Lord and Savior Jesus Christ
whose Holy Spirit imparted
supernatural knowledge to me
during my fifteen years of studying
the issues presented here
and to the memory of
my wonderful wife, Theda,
who was with me through
the many trials and tribulations
it took to complete the
experiential research
necessary to produce this work.

And to the marvelous, dedicated researchers, too
numerous to mention.

"Where the spirit of the Lord is there is liberty."
2 Corinthians 3:17

This is the greatest "How to"
book of the 21st century!
Nothing like it has ever been written.

NOTE: For those of you who enjoy pointing out mistakes, I have scattered enough of them throughout this book to keep you happy. I expect that "the nattering nabobs of negativism" will be thoroughly vilifying my work and all I can offer in defense is

AVOIDING ALL CRITICISM IS EASY—
SIMPLY SAY NOTHING, DO NOTHING
AND BE NOTHING.

Bob Plimpton

TABLE OF CONTENTS

Introduction   i–xii

MYTH ONE–
You must have a birth certificate   1

MYTH TWO–
You must have a social security number   7

MYTH THREE–
You need a marriage license   12

MYTH FOUR–
You own your vehicles   17

MYTH FIVE–
You must pay an income tax   26

MYTH SIX–
You must obey all "laws"   36

MYTH SEVEN–
We have courts of justice   39

MYTH EIGHT–
Banks loan money   45

MYTH NINE–
You should have a will   55

MYTH TEN–
You should incorporate your business   60

Uniform Commercial
   Code (UCC) Explained   63

Appendix   68

TEN MODERN MYTHS THAT HAVE NO BASIS— BUSTED!

Introduction

Exactly who *are* you? Very few of us have any idea who we really are. We have been taught since birth to go along with a great many laws, rules, regulations, and ordinances that really have nothing to do with us but only apply to who we *think* and *presume* that we are. They are really only MYTHS!

Look in your wallet or purse and you will notice that the name on all your credit cards, insurance cards, club cards, and driver's license is in ALL CAPITAL LETTERS. That is not you! That is known as your STRAW MAN.

In 1938 the United States Supreme Court, in *Erie Railroad v. Tompkins,* changed our justice system from one of public *law* to one of public *policy* and determined that everything is in Commerce. That took away our constitutional rights replacing them with corporate government rules and regulations. Governments and courts are not real; they are *corporate fictions.* In today's "courts" we are now guilty until proven innocent because the government *presumes* that we are *juristic, corporate* persons subject to its laws, rules, regulations, and ordinances.

However, *unlike entities* cannot be joined in Commerce. If you cut corporations, governments, courts or banks, they do not bleed. They are fictitious. If you get cut, you *do* bleed. You are real. You and the government are *unlike entities* and cannot be joined in Commerce. You are *real*, they are *fictitious.*

So, our government corporations created and offered to us the STRAW MAN as the *optional* commercial instrument/entity to enable us to move and operate in Commerce, referenced as an act of commercial intercourse, and changed us into "corporations" so they could do business with us in Commerce. They invented the STRAW MAN, our name in ALL CAPITAL LETTERS—a fictitious entity, a corporation!

> STRAW MAN. *A "front"; a third party who is put up in name only to take part in a transaction. Nominal party to a transaction; one who acts as an agent for another for the purpose of taking title to real prop-*

*erty and executing whatever documents
and instruments the principal may direct
respecting the property. Person who purchases
property for another to conceal identity of
real purchaser, or to accomplish some purpose
otherwise not allowed.*

(Black's Law Dictionary, 6th ed.)

Are you beginning to get an idea of who you really are and not who you have always thought you are? You are a living, breathing soul—a child of Yahweh! You have God given rights which are protected by the Constitution, the corporate *citizens'* "civil rights" are granted by government and are called privileges, they can be taken away by government at any time. For example, living souls have the right to keep and bear arms; citizens, in the "colorable" sense of the word by which government operates in relation to you and me, have no such right. "Colorable" is a bona fide legal term for the many frauds government commits against us.

You were *born* free and sovereign. That is called your LEGAL STATUS. Then you moved from SOVEREIGN LEGAL STATUS to ALL CONTRACTUAL by entering into a series of contracts. This started with your well-intentioned parents' inadvertent recording of your birth certificate with the government. Most people are not aware of it, but no law requires that! The voluntary and never denied aspects of your status is what clinches the government's nonexistent claim over your entire life and person, as will be explained as we proceed.

Then you signed an application for a Social Security number (no law requires that).

Then you signed an application for a driver's license (no law requires that).

Then you signed an application for voter registration (no law requires that).

Then you signed an application for a marriage license (no law requires that unless you wish to intermarry, marry a person of a different race).

Then you signed a license to engage in your business or occupation (no law requires that).

Then you signed a Form 1040 and filed it with the IRS (no law requires that).

Then you signed an application for a permit to build a house, enter into business, collect rents, or whatever else you were asked to do (no law requires any of that).

All of the above acts were *voluntary* on your part and *fraudulent* on the state's part. That is because you were not fully informed of their implications, but you can avoid them all **if you know the rules of the game!**

> *"Resistance to tyrants is obedience to God."*
>
> (Thomas Jefferson)

Now when I state that "no law requires that" I specifically mean that no law *which applies to you* requires that. All laws apply to corporate beings but you can rebut the presumption that you are a corporate being.

Because of the corporate entity known as our STRAW MAN, e.g. JOHN HENRY DOE, the *presumption* of government and the courts is that we are juristic, corporate beings and not living, breathing souls. But that is a *rebuttable presumption*.

> REBUTTABLE PRESUMPTION. *In the law of evidence, a presumption which may be rebutted by evidence. Otherwise called a "disputable" presumption. A species of legal presumption which holds good until evidence contrary to it is introduced.*
>
> (Black's Law Dictionary, 6th ed.)

All that is required in order to rebut the presumption that we are juristic, corporate beings subject to all the laws, rules, regulations, statutes, and ordinances governmental authorities have thought up in order to gain control over us, is to serve them with an Affidavit of Denial of Corporate Status and a Notice of Copyright of our STRAW MAN. That completely rebuts the presumption that you are a juristic, corporate being and any court, or other "controlling authority" is DEAD. It cannot move forward at all and you have won your case.

So? What good does that do?

Well, it means that you can do anything you want to on or with your own property as long as you cause no injury or property damage to your neighbors or anyone else. You are not subject to building codes, zoning laws, architectural committee rules, city ordinances, property taxes, homeowners association rules, regulations or whatever.

All those laws, rules, regulations, ordinances and codes you have always thought applied to you applied only because *you let them apply.* You did not know who you are nor how to rebut the presumption that you are a juristic, corporate being subject to whatever rules and regulations any government corporation wishes to use to control you.

Look at it this way; if you go to work for any corporation, whether it be a company or a government entity, you are given a handbook of corporate rules. Those rules usually dictate the hours you will work, the office or station you will occupy, the company dress code, parking regulations, time clock etiquette, use of expense accounts or vouchers, ID tags and other corporate rules and regulations.

All the rules and regulations apply to you because of your contract with your employer. However, if an outsider, someone not under employment contract to the corporation, visits the facility, do the corporate rules and regulations apply to them?

Not at all—and that is the way it is in the world of Commerce. Everything is done according to contract.

History

We were all created by God who is sovereign. The creator has authority and control over the creation so at birth we are subject only to God. Our status is that of *free* men and women. Previous free men and women created government so *we* have authority and control over government in the same way that God has authority and control over us. Then government created corporations over which the government has authority and control. (See MYTH TEN, *You should incorporate your business.*) Then government incorporated itself. *Then they incorporated us so they could interface with and have control over us!*

Yes, the United States is a *municipal corporation* as is every state, county, city, town, village, property owners association, etc. (Municipal entities come within the exclusive purview of Admiralty Law.) The UNITED STATES (municipal corporation) has exclusive jurisdiction over only the ten square miles of the District of Columbia, any territories such as Guam and Puerto Rico, and military installations such as shipyards, military bases, federal courthouses, U.S. post offices, etc. and, by adoption under the Uniform Laws of the U.S. Corporation, the various state legislatures voluntarily subject the people of the states to *federal process.*

However, there are *two* federal governments! First is the united States of America formed by free men and women, living souls, operating under the Constitution which was written for it. The other is the incorporated united States with no constitution, only by-laws, rules and regulations. Congress, the House of Representatives and the Senate, make laws for *both* of these governments, but they have *exclusive jurisdiction* only over the UNITED STATES corporation and not over the united States of America or the individual sovereign states and people.

They can pass any legislation they wish pertaining to the united States corporation but must adhere to the Constitution when passing laws pertaining to the united States of America and the various sovereign states. If a law is passed that is unconstitutional, it applies only to the people who live, were born or do business in the municipal UNITED STATES and not to those in the united States of America! But, of course, not knowing any better, we presume that every law passed pertains to us wherever we live, work or do business.

So we "ignorantly" traverse into *adhesion contracts* (the legal term for these connections) which change us from free men of STATUS to men under contract or

agreement, *corporate beings* subject to whatever laws, rules, regulations, or ordinances,
the *corporate governments* wish to place on
us. Some of these adhesion contracts are:

Birth certificates
    Social Security applications
        DMV registration of our vehicles
        Driver's licenses
          Voter registration
           Marriage licenses
           Business licenses

    In fact, government has created a com-
mercial STRAW MAN for each of us so we
can operate in Commerce as corporations.
Each of our STRAW MEN *are* corporations which are subject to their creator, the
STATE. The personal corporation they created for each of us is our own name in ALL
CAPITAL LETTERS, for example JOHN
HENRY DOE. Remember . . . they can't
reach, or do business with us directly, only
indirectly with a large portion of *presumption* as their additional source of power.
    However, despite those adhesion con-
tracts, we are still sovereign over the agencies which we created as evidenced by

California Government Code, Sections 11120 and 54950 which both state: *"The people of this State do not yield their sovereignty to the agencies which serve them."* The federal Constitution and that of every state affirm the same thing.

We, individually and corporately, are SOVEREIGN over government agencies of whatever kind or make, except that many of the agencies are not registered with the Secretary of State to do business in the state and exist as unincorporated associations that can't be sued. In Oregon, for example, the state police are not a registered corporation! You are well-advised to check out the agencies of your own state government.

So the answer to the question "Who are you?" is that you are SOVEREIGN! You are in fact a SOVEREIGN that *has the liberty to enter into contract.* The issue of Commerce and contract *is where the traps and snares wait for you* but, contrary to what you may have always thought, that changes everything!

Bob Plimpton
North Palm Beach, Florida
April 15, 2004

Note: Each of the ten MYTHS reviewed here could be, or could have been, expanded upon, some *ad infinitum,* but I wanted to make this work an easy read which succinctly presents the issues and lets the reader take it from there. A word to the wise is, as they say, sufficient.

Disclaimer: I am not an attorney. Neither I nor The Boaz Trust give or sell legal advice. Ours is strictly an educational effort. We merely present the facts and the law. If you feel you need further help, contact The Boaz Trust. If you feel you need legal advice, by all means see an attorney.

MYTH ONE—*You must have a birth certificate*

"Like it or not, you are a slave."
Dr. Alan Keyes

Are we owned by the government?

In 1921, the federal Sheppard-Towner Maternity Act created birth registration or what we now know as the "birth certificate." It was sold to the American people as a law that would reduce maternal and infant mortality, protect the health of mothers and infants, and to accomplish "other purposes."

One of those other purposes provided for state agencies in the overseeing of their operations and expenditures. What it *really* did was create a federal "birth registry" which exists today, creating FEDERAL CHILDREN. This government of "Parens Patriae," now legislates for American children as if they are owned by the federal or state government. Through the public school enrollment process and continuing license requirements for most aspects of daily life, these children grow up to be adults indoctrinated into those things necessary to carry out activities that exist in what is called a free country.

Before 1921, the records of births and names of children were entered into the family Bibles, as were the records of marriages, deaths and other family events. Both the family and the law readily accepted these records as official. Since 1921, the American people have been registering the births and names of their children with the government of the county and state in which they are born, even though *there is no law requiring it.* The state tells you that registering your child's birth through the birth certificate serves as proof that he/she was born in the United States, thereby making him/her a United States citizen. For the past several years a social security number was mandated to be issued at birth by the federal government. The social security number is one of those "other purposes." It serves as a means of lifelong tracking of the one whose name is on the birth certificate.

On April 9, 1933, the United States corporation was declared bankrupt by President Roosevelt. Visit *www.freedomdomain.com/ bankrupt.html* for the full details. The governors of the then forty-eight states pledged the constitutional "full faith and credit" of each of their states, including the citizenry as collateral, for loans of credit from the privately owned Federal Reserve bank.

> FULL FAITH AND CREDIT. *The clause of the U.S. Constitution (Article IV, Section I) which provides the various states must recognize legislative acts, public records, and judicial decisions of the other states within the united States. It requires that foreign judgment be given such faith and credit as it had by law or usage of state of its origin and that foreign statutes are to have force and effect to which they are entitled in the home state. And that judgment of record shall have the same FAITH, CREDIT, CONCLUSIVE EFFECT AND OBLIGATORY FORCE in other states as it has by law or usage in the state from whence taken.*
>
> (Black's Law Dictionary, 6th ed.)

After receiving the information of live birth and other particulars for the birth certificate accompanied by the assigned social security number, *the state claims an interest in every child within its jurisdiction*. The state will, if it deems it necessary, nullify your parental rights and appoint a guardian (trustee, foster parent) over what you thought were *your* children. The subject of every birth certificate is a child. The child is a valuable asset that, if properly trained, can contribute valuable assets provided by its labor for many years. It is presumed by those who have researched this issue, that the child itself is the asset of the trust established by the birth certificate, and the social security number is the numbering registration of the trust, allowing for the trust's assets to be tracked so our children are owned by the state. Each one of us, including our children, is considered an asset of the bankrupt United States corporation. We are now designated by this government as "HUMAN RESOURCES," born in a DELIVERY room, delivered to the state of birth by way of the *BIRTH CERTIFICATE* for which our INFORMER (our mother) provides the requested information including the NAME and SOCIAL SECURITY (or tracking) NUMBER wherewith this bankrupt government is supplied with a new crop of COLLATERAL born each year.

After being born free men and women, our parents inadvertently turn us over to the state by recording a birth certificate with the county in which we were born. We are then chattel and our lifetime production is to be used against the bankruptcy of the incorporated municipal UNITED STATES. The certificate is sent to the Department of Commerce, where the government keeps track of its property, and is credited to the privately owned Federal Reserve bank which is not federal, has no reserves and is not a bank but is privately owned by twelve unimaginably wealthy families. Visit *www.elimadebts.com* for the full sad story of the Federal Reserve Bank.

Your birth certificate is valued at $1 million, which is what the government has decided, on average, each individual will produce during their lifetime and is used by the government as collateral to borrow money for various purposes.

The birth certificate, in effect, says to the government "Oh Master, sir, here's another slave for you to work on your plantation." The parents, being slaves themselves, do not own the children, the government (Old Master) owns them, for it was he who gave the parents *permission to marry* (marriage license) and, if the parents do not take care of his children and treat them properly, the state *Social Services* will take them away and place them elsewhere.

MYTH BUSTED!

There is no law which says a birth certificate must be made out at all. The birth of a child was traditionally recorded in the family Bible and that was that. If that is done, and many are doing so as this knowledge spreads, *there is no obligation for the person to perform for the government in any way.* One can make out a Certificate of Birth for the newborn, can even use the state's form, just *do not file it with the county* if you wish your children to remain free men and women. For complete information order CD #1 "How to avoid the birth certificate trap."

FREEDOM IS *FUN!*

MYTH TWO—*You must have a social security number*

Parents submit an application for a social security number (SSN) for the newborn baby or one is applied for shortly thereafter. This is an adhesion contract which further obligates a new citizen to the government.

The SSN is the "consideration" for the international banking cartel to collateralize our ability to produce goods, services and acquire wealth into the indefinite future as "a derivative" to float the public debt.

MYTH BUSTED!

About Social Security:
"When you pay social security taxes, you are in no way making provision for your own retirement. You are paying the pensions of those who are already retired. Once you understand this, you see that whether you will get the benefits you are counting on when you retire depends on whether Congress

will levy enough taxes, borrow enough, or print enough money. . . ."

(W. Allen Wallis, former Chairman of the 1975 Advisory Council on Social Security)

"There is no prospect that today's younger workers will receive all the Social Security and Medicare benefits currently promised them."

(Dorcas Hardy, former Social Security Commissioner, qted. in *Reader's Digest,* Dec., 1995.)

"All we have to do now is to inform the public that the payment of social security taxes is voluntary and watch the mass exodus."

(Walter E. Williams, Professor of Economics, George Mason University)

The above quotes courtesy of Joseph Farah, *www.worldnetdaily.com.*

There is no law which says *anyone* must apply for a social security number. It is entirely voluntary and, contrary to public opinion, employers cannot deny employment to anyone who does not have an SSN nor can any other services be denied by anyone for lack of an SSN. Not to say it will not happen but if it does it is illegal and can be sued upon.

Title V of United States, Code Annotated 552 (a) is known as The Privacy Act of 1974. Based on the Privacy Act, "It is against the law to require a common numerical identifier such as a social security or other number for any purpose when the individual does not wish to disclose one, they must still receive the right, benefit or privilege afforded by law as others would receive by disclosing a common numerical identifier."

Courts have ruled in part:

"Right of privacy is a personal right designed to protect persons from unwanted disclosure of personal information. . . ."

(I Financial Corporation v. Local 743)

The District Court in Delaware held that The Privacy Act:

"was enacted for the purpose of curtailing the expanding use of social security numbers . . . and to eliminate the threat to individual privacy and confidentiality of

*information posed by common numerical
identifiers."*

(*Doyle v. Wilson, D.C.*)

Should any person, business or government agency decide to deny individuals any right, benefit or privilege when they refuse to reveal a social security number or other common numerical identifier, individuals can file summary suits in U.S. District Court, and if successful, are assured a *minimum* of $1,000 plus attorney fees:

(A) actual damages sustained by the individual as a result of the refusal or failure, but in no case shall a person entitled to recovery receive less than the sum of $1,000.00; and
(B) the costs of the action together with reasonable attorney fees as determined by the court.

Courts have determined that only the Department of Social Services and the IRS are permitted access to your social security account number. The IRS is not a U.S. government agency. It is a private collection agency for the International Monetary

Fund (IMF), as stated in *Diversified Metal Products v. IRS et al.*

Call 800-TAX-NOMO and buy a copy of *The Social Security Scam* by Irwin Schiff. For complete information on social security order CD #2 "How to avoid the social security trap."

FREEDOM IS *FUN!*

MYTH THREE—*You need a marriage license*

> "MARRIAGE LICENSE. *A license or permission granted by public authority to persons who intend to intermarry. . . .*"
>
> Black's Law Dictionary, 6th ed.

Did you get that? If you wish to marry a person of another race, you need a state issued marriage license. Otherwise, under law, you do not.

MYTH BUSTED!

The marriage license is a state TRAP! When you marry *anyone* with a state issued marriage license, the state becomes a third party to the marriage and, since the state issued the license and gave permission for the marriage, it has the highest interest in and control over the marriage and any offspring.

When you get a marriage license from the state, you become slaves to Old Master who gave you *permission to marry*. On the old plantation, when two slaves were given permission to marry, whose children were the offspring? They did not belong to the slaves, they were the property of Old Master and it is that way today.

That is why Social Services can take your children away from you if they even *think*, or someone reports, that you are not treating them in a proper manner. They are not your children, they belong to Old Master.

You do not need a marriage license to get married. It is your God-given right to marry. The state cannot take away your God-given rights *but* you can voluntarily give them up by applying for and obtaining a state marriage license, driver's license, business license or any other state issued license. With a state marriage license you cannot be joined in Holy Matrimony you can only be married in a church. Do you suppose that has anything to do with the alarming divorce rate in America today?

However, the state is looking for CONTROL. So, in the case of marriage, they very cleverly set things up so that most churches cannot marry a couple without a state marriage license. How did they do that?

All churches and ministries are exempt from taxation and money given to them is deductible from income taxes, if one is ignorant enough or timid enough to still be paying such extortion to the IRS. (See MYTH SIX.) The IRS even acknowledges that fact in Section 508(c)(1) of the Internal Revenue Code which says that churches and ministries are *mandated* to be exempt. Visit www.hushmoney.org for the complete story.

To solve the state's "problem" and gain control of the people, the state sent their agents, called attorneys and CPAs, into the field to tell churches that they must file for 501(c)(3) corporate status if they want to be able to issue tax receipts to their donors. The churches really didn't have to. It was all a deception, otherwise known as a lie, but that is the way those state agents operate— for the good of the state and to foment trouble which means attorney and CPA fees later on.

So nearly all the churches fell for the lie, fell into the MYTH and became 501(c)(3) corporate STATE AGENCIES. They sold their birthrights for a mess of pottage! A

501(c)(3) church is no longer a church of Jesus Christ but is a *state agency*! Now, since they are state agencies, they must obey state laws, rules, regulations, ordinances, zoning and building codes and other regulatory encroachments. Their property belongs to the state which can confiscate it if they misbehave or if the state even *considers* that they are misbehaving and they must hire only state licensed teachers for their church schools and pretty much tow whatever mark the state mandates. One of the cardinal rules is that a church's members *must* have a state marriage license or that church, being a state agency, is forbidden to marry them.

For centuries all that was required for a union in holy matrimony was a written covenant between the two parties with witnesses and cohabitation. If they wanted a preacher or justice of the peace to perform a ceremony, all well and good, but there was no state marriage license required. The marriage was recorded in the family Bible and the offspring belonged to the people, who raised them largely in the admonition of the Lord and thus was established the solid foundation on which was built the most blessed, prosperous and free nation in history!

Then the state sought control.

Couples may still be united in Holy Matrimony either by signing a covenant between them in front of two or more witnesses and cohabitating or finding a "free" church or preacher to perform a ceremony without a state license. The Holy Matrimony is then recorded in the family Bible, the covenant certificate filed away and that is that.

In that case the state has no jurisdiction over the marriage and cannot take the children from the parents for any reason. For complete information regarding marriage licenses visit *www.hushmoney.org* then order CD #3 "How to avoid the marriage license trap."

(Note: all CDs are only files sent by e-mail as attachments. We call them *electronic CDs.*)

FREEDOM IS *FUN!*

MYTH FOUR—*You own your vehicles*

When you purchase a vehicle you must let the dealer handle the tags and title for you and get you a certificate of title from the Department of Motor Vehicles (DMV) and registration plates for the vehicle. The dealer will send all the papers, including the Manufacturer's Certificate of Origin to the DMV and you will get back a Certificate of Title, evidencing mere color of title and purportedly showing you own the vehicle.

MYTH BUSTED!

The Lord Himself busted this MYTH as follows:

In 1982 I was happily retired from business and was mowing my lawn in Palm Beach County, Florida, minding my own business, when I heard from the Lord: "Get involved in the governmental process."

"I know nothing about the governmental process," I said.

"That's alright, *I* do," said the Lord.

Realizing that He surely did know about the governmental process, having invented it, I asked what He wanted me to do. The rest is history. For over twenty years He has given me firsthand, hands-on experience and teachings that have resulted in complete financial and regulatory freedom unlike that of anyone else I know.

Folks have a difficult time believing the way I live. For example, I have two vehicles, a 2001 VW and a 2003 Chrysler which are *privately owned*, require no registration, insurance or a driver's license to use them and they cannot be taxed or liened. God supernaturally taught me how to get into that enviable position. Let me explain.

In 1996 I bought a double-wide mobile home for use as a ranch manager's cottage at a Christian retreat we were developing. I was paying cash and, as I signed the agreement to purchase, the Lord said to me, "You get the MCO." I had no idea what an MCO was, I had never heard the expression but, since He said it, I repeated it and told the salesman, "I get the MCO." He said, "OK." Of course I rushed out to learn that an MCO is the Manufacturer's Certificate of Origin. It is the actual birth certificate of the vehicle. It is the TITLE to the vehicle!

At the closing our conversation went like this:

Me: Remember, I get the MCO.
Salesman: No, the MCO goes to the DMV.
Me: No, remember when I signed the agreement to purchase, I told you I get the MCO.
Salesman: No, the MCO goes to the DMV.
Me: Show me the regulations.

He gave me the regulations. I took my wife to lunch, flipped open the regulations to the sixth page and there was Section 20 which says, "The first purchaser of a vehicle from any dealer gets the Manufacturer's Certificate of Origin (MCO) unless the vehicle is being financed in which case the MCO goes to the Department of Motor Vehicles (DMV) which holds it as a third party against the indebtedness on the vehicle."

I took the regulations back to the salesman who was dumbfounded and said:

Salesman: I never heard of such a thing.
Me: Well, how many of your customers pay cash?
Salesman: About a third.
Me: Well, they should all be getting the MCO.

Salesman: I will have to call the president of Fleetwood Homes (manufacturer of the mobile home I was buying).

He called the president and told him what I wanted.

President: No, the MCO goes to the DMV.
Salesman: Let me fax you something.

He faxed Section 20 to the president and called him about twenty minutes later.

Salesman: Did you get the fax?
President: Yes.
Salesman: What does it say?
President: It says he gets the MCO.
Salesman: Well, do I give it to him?
President: Let me call the head of the DMV in Raleigh (This was in NC.).

The president later told me that when he called the head of the DMV and explained the situation, the conversation went like this:

DMV: No, *we* get the MCO.
President: Look at Section 20 of the Regs. What does it say?

DMV: It says *he* gets the MCO.
President: Well, do I give it to him?
DMV: I guess so!

Think of that! Do you realize what you just read? None of the professionals had any idea of the actual facts! They had been doing things wrong for so long, they thought it was right!

But God knew and supernaturally imparted the knowledge to me which is the manner in which He has imparted everything The Boaz Trust does.

OK, so much for that. Now, what's the big deal about who gets the MCO for a vehicle? Well, the MCO, as I have said, is the birth certificate or title to the vehicle. Once it is turned over to the DMV, the state owns the vehicle and the DMV issues the so-called owner of the vehicle a Certificate of Title meaning that there is a title somewhere. The state has it and owns the vehicle! The person who considers himself the owner of the vehicle merely has *beneficial use* of the vehicle and may only use said state vehicle if they follow the REAL owner's rules to wit:

a) Get a state registration (license plate) so the state can keep track of its property.

b) Insure the vehicle so the state's property is protected from damage and responsibility.

c) Obtain a driver's license so the state knows that only state qualified people are driving their vehicle.

d) Pay rent (taxes) to the state in exchange for beneficial use of the vehicle.

Now, since I have the MCOs for my vehicles, these rules do not apply to me. No law says I must register MY property with the state, the state cannot force me into a contract with a third party (insurance) regarding MY property, I do not need a driver's license to travel in my private conveyance, but I use the highways as a matter of right. I don't need it but I actually carry an International Driving Permit (IDP). The state cannot charge me rent (tax) for my personally owned goods. They do not even know that the vehicles exist since the MCOs were given directly to me and I do not owe them "rent" for the use of MY vehicles.

I actually have each vehicle titled to a separate Pure Trust. That way, should I ever desire to sell, I need not sell the vehicle, only the Trust and the buyer enjoys the same benefits I have enjoyed. Or I can get a state title and sell the vehicle, buyer's choice. You can do the same with aircraft, boats or any other vehicle.

The law says "Any dealer transferring title to a new vehicle shall deliver the Manufacturer's Certificate of Origin (MCO), duly signed, to the transferee at the time of delivering the vehicle. . . ." (North Carolina General Statutes Chapter 20, Sec. 20-52.1.) However, when the vehicle is being financed, the MCO goes to the Department of Motor Vehicles (DMV) which holds it as a third party for the protection of the lender. This is true in every state.

As this knowledge spreads, more and more people paying cash for a new vehicle are demanding the MCO from the dealer and maintaining complete private ownership of their vehicles. *They use no driver's license at all.* Instead of a vehicle registration plate, they use a dealer's vanity plate. (See photo of my two vehicles.)

They do not insure their vehicle(s) because they depend on the supernatural protection of the Lord to prevent any and all accidents. It is scriptural that *we* are responsible for our own actions. When we turn that responsibility over to an insurance company, we move out from under the supernatural protection of the almighty. *There are no accidents with God.* There can be many without Him.

They never pay taxes on the vehicle because the state doesn't own it and does not know it exists. No "rent" is due. They cannot be given "tickets" (summons) because they have not accepted either a driver's license or certificate of title. California Vehicle Code (CVC) 17459 states, "The acceptance by a resident of this state of a certificate of title or ownership or a certificate of registration of any motor vehicle . . . shall constitute the consent by the person that service of summons may be made upon him within or without this state. . . ."

Did you get that one? No registration, no tickets for parking, double parking, running red lights or stops signs, speeding or anything else. This is true in every state.

And CVC 17460 states, "The acceptance or retention by a resident of this state of a driver's license . . . shall constitute the consent of the person that service of summons may be made upon him within or without this state." Did you get that? No driver's license, no tickets! The cop does not have your consent! Every state has this.

Of course, as good Christian people we are to conduct ourselves circumspectly and not put ourselves in a position of causing bodily injury or property damage to anyone at any time. COOL IT!

My Two Cars

FREEDOM IS *FUN!*

MYTH FIVE—*You must pay an income tax*

"Like it or not, you are a slave. You admit you are a slave every April 15th! That's when you sign forms that 'voluntarily' lay bare to the government the most private details of your life! Few people realize the income tax is a slave tax. It can never be compatible with the life of a free people."

Dr. Alan Keyes

"Render unto Caesar that which is Caesar's and to God that which is God's."

Jesus Christ quoted in Matthew 22:21, Mark 12:17 and Luke 20:25

Every year millions of Americans fill out a Form 1040 and submit it to the IRS along with many of their hard earned dollars or to get a 'rebate' on money the IRS has previously extorted from them. We are all told that we must do so if we "earned" more than some artificial threshold established internally by the IRS. The government-controlled media publishes all manner of false information about the income tax being mandatory and the vast majority of the senators and congressmen go along with the charade like gutless sheep.

MYTH BUSTED!

Power over a man's substance amounts to power over his will.

(Alexander Hamilton)

When you fill out a Form 1040 and file it with the IRS, where do you think your money goes? You probably think that it goes toward paying for governmental services of one kind or another, correct? However, you are *wrong*! Every cent you send to the IRS is used to make payment of principal and interest to the *privately owned* Federal Reserve bank against the *artificially created* bankruptcy of the municipal corporate United States.

Wait a cotton pickin' minute! Did I say the UNITED STATES corporation is bankrupt? Yes gentle reader, it is sad but true that on April 9, 1933, President Franklin D. Roosevelt declared the UNITED STATES *bankrupt*!

Visit *www.freedomdomain.com/bankrupt. html* for the full details.

Why? What happened? Well, in 1913 our wonderful elected U.S. senators passed the Federal Reserve Act on December 23. This unconscionable and unconstitutional act turned the money system of the country over to the privately owned Federal Reserve Bank (FRB). Visit *www.elimadebts. com* for the full story of the fraudulent FRB.

The Federal Reserve Act was passed on December 23, 1913 with only twelve senators present. The vote was unanimous so their names did not have to be recorded. The FRB then called in the debt of the government which had borrowed huge amounts of money from the bankster families. But the government could not pay.

So the FRB, being the benevolent soul it is, not only agreed to forego foreclosure at that time but granted a twenty-year moratorium on principal and interest. The banksters well knew that the greedy politicians would go on a spending spree. That is what financed the Roaring Twenties!

Then twenty years later, 1933, came the day of reckoning when the country was totally unable to pay the *artificially created* debt to the FRB. Bankrupt we were and our benevolent government pledged its assets, *you and me and our productivity for life* to the FRB in payment toward the principal and interest of the bankruptcy! At that point we all became indentured slaves on the plantation run by the FRB, the International Money Fund (IMF) and the world banksters' interest.

All money collected by the IRS, which is a private collection agency for the International Monetary Fund (IMF) through the FRB, *Diversified Metal Product v. IRS et al.*, CV-93-405E-EJE U.S.D.C.D.I., Public Law 94-564, Senate Report 94-1148 pg 5967, goes toward the principal and interest of the bankruptcy and NOT ONE DIME goes to support any governmental program of any kind. Doesn't that make you happy?

The IRS admits that there are over thirty-three million non-filers of the Form 1040. There is no law which says that anyone but a federal employee must fill out a Form 1040 or any other form and file it with the IRS unless they are involved in the manufacture, sale or distribution of alcohol, tobacco and firearms or engaged in "wagering."

Some folks claim that the income tax is unconstitutional but that is incorrect. If it were *mandatory* it would be unconstitutional but since it is *voluntary*, it is not because while government cannot take away our God-given rights, we can **voluntarily** give them up by signing a Form 1040 or other form with the IRS!

Read what past IRS Commissioners had to say about it:

> *Each year American taxpayers **voluntarily** file their tax returns and make a special effort to pay the taxes they owe.*
>
> (Johnnie M. Walters IRS Commissioner, Internal Revenue 1040 Booklet, 1971)

> *Our tax system is based on individual self-assessment and **voluntary** compliance.*
>
> (Mortimer Caplin, IRS Commissioner, Internal Revenue Audit Manual, 1975)

> *There is no doubt that better taxpayer assistance, more sensitive responsiveness to taxpayer complaints and problems and simpler tax forms and instructions are of great*

*importance in achieving a high level of **vol-untary** compliance with our tax laws.*

(Jerome Kurtz, IRS Commissioner, 1979)

*The IRS's primary task is to collect taxes under a **voluntary** compliance system.*

(Jerome Kurtz, IRS Commissioner,
Annual Report, 1980)

*Thank you for participating in the world's most successful **voluntary** income tax system.*

(Margaret Richardson, IRS Commissioner,
IRS 1040 Booklet, 1985)

*Two aspects of the Federal income tax system—**voluntary** compliance with the law and self assessment of tax—make it impor-tant for you to understand your rights and responsibilities as a taxpayer. Voluntary compliance places on the taxpayer the responsibility for filing an income tax return. **You** must decide whether the law requires you to file a return. If it does, you must file your return by the date it is due.*

(IRS Publication #21)

And what does the United States Supreme Court have to say about it? Read the following United States Supreme Court cases regarding the personal income tax:

THE INCOME TAX IS **VOLUNTARY**
Flora v. U.S., 362 U.S. 145 (1960)

COMPENSATION IS A DIRECT ITEM OF
   INCOME NOT TAXABLE BY THE
   FEDERAL GOVERNMENT
United States Constitution, Art. I
Pollack v. Farmers Loan & Trust Co., 158 U.S.
   601 at 637 (1895)
Knowlton v. Moore, 178 U.S. 41 (1900)

THE SIXTEENTH AMENDMENT AND THE
   INCOME TAX IS LIMITED TO *INDIRECT*
   EXCISE TAXES
Brushaber v. Union Pacific RR Co., 240 U.S. 1 at
   10, 11, 12, 19 (1916)
Eisner v. Macomber, 252 U.S. 189 at 205 (1920)
Peck v. Lowe, 247 U.S. 163 (1918)
Stanton v. Baltic Mining Co., 240 U.S. 103 (1916)
Flint v. Stone Tracy Co., 220 U.S. 153, 165 (1911)

INCOME IS PROFITS AND GAINS MADE
   THROUGH THE SALE OR CONVERSION
   OF A CAPITAL ASSET
Eisner v. Macomber, 252 U.S. 189 at 205 (1920)
Conner v. U.S., 303 F. Supp. 1187 pg 119 (1968)
Doyle v. Mitchell Brothers, 247 U.S. 179 (1916)

THE RIGHT TO LABOR IN AN
 UNREGULATED OCCUPATION IS *A
 FUNDAMENTAL RIGHT* AND NOT A
 TAXABLE PRIVILEGE
Murdock v. Pennsylvania, 319 U.S. 105 at
 113 (1943)
Butchers Union Co. v. Crescent City Co., 111 U.S.
 746 at 756–767 (1884)
Coppage v. Kansas, 236 U.S. 1 at 14 (1916)
Meyer v. Nebraska, 262 U.S. 390, 399, 400 (1923)

But don't people go to jail for not paying their taxes? Yes, many have gone to jail
for "willful failure to file" but only because
they were unfamiliar with the court system.
See MYTH EIGHT—We have courts of
justice. If one is familiar with the way in
which our so-called courts of justice operate, one is *assured* of winning against the
IRS and a great many have done so.

My people perish for lack of knowledge.
(Hosea 4:6)

The IRS claims that they always win but
they LIE. They don't want anyone to know
how many times they have lost or their
bluff might be called and their scam
exposed. For excellent information about

the income tax scam enter "Otto Skinner" or "Larken Rose" in your internet search engine window and be prepared to learn a great deal of truth.

When you file a Form 1040 with the IRS, you have signed, under penalty of perjury, that you owe them the money YOU have stated (self-assessment) and you (voluntarily) give up your God-given, constitutionally protected right against giving testimony against yourself in a criminal matter (Fifth Amendment) and give the IRS jurisdiction over you. You better not "fudge" or make a mistake for then you are in big trouble as Leona Helmsley and a great many others have found out.

However, if you *do not file*, the IRS has no jurisdiction over you whatever and there is NO LAW requiring you to file unless you are a federal employee. A word to the wise is sufficient!

Imagine the joy of not having to keep receipts, hire an accountant or pay anything to the IRS which is actually a *private collection agency* for the IMF through the FRB *Diversified Metal Product v. IRS et al.*, (CV-93-405E-EJE U.S.D.C.D.I., Public Law 94-564, Senate Report 94-1148 pg 5967) and the private banking interests of the twelve unimaginably wealthy "families" who own the FRB, the IMF and really control the world including our legislators in the House and Senate! Visit *www.elimadebts. com* for the full sad story of the Federal Reserve Bank.

For complete information about the income tax hoax, hear it from a former director of the Internal Revenue Service Criminal Investigation Division, Joe Bannister, and visit *www.freedomabovefortune. com*. You will learn more than you ever wanted to know about the income tax and why *you do not owe it!*

As for me and my house, we will serve the Lord and no other. April 15 each year is just another sunny day for me and my family. My wife and I go out to a marvelous dinner to celebrate our freedom from the skullduggery of the FRB through the IRS.

For all the forms needed to stop paying income taxes order Electronic CD #5 "How to legally stop paying income taxes."

FREEDOM IS *FUN!*

MYTH SIX—*You must obey all "laws"*

The vast majority, if not all, of us have believed for years that we must obey all the laws, rules, regulations, ordinances, government codes, etc. that any legislature, county, city or other government agency makes up to control our actions. THAT IS TRUE but only because we do not know who we are.

We are sovereign over the government agencies of which we, the living, breathing people collectively, are co-creators. California Government Code, Section 100 states, "The people of this state did not give up their Sovereignty over the agencies which they created." That is true in every state.

The *presumption* of government and the courts is that we are juristic, *corporate beings* and not living, breathing souls. But that is a *rebuttable presumption.*

REBUTTABLE PRESUMPTION. *In the law of evidence, a presumption which may be rebutted by evidence. Otherwise called a "disputable" presumption. A species of legal presumption which holds good until evidence contrary to it is introduced.*

(Black's Law Dictionary, 6th ed.)

MYTH BUSTED!

All that is required in order to rebut the presumption that we are juristic, corporate beings is to serve the plaintiff's attorney and the clerk of the court in which you are being sued with an Affidavit of Denial of Corporate Status and a Notice of Copyright of your STRAW MAN.

That completely rebuts the presumption that you are a juristic, corporate being and the court is DEAD. It cannot move forward at all and you have won your case or cause.

Federal Rules of Civil Procedure, Sec. III, Motions and Pleadings, Rule 9(a) states in pertinent part:

"When an issue is raised as to the *legal existence of a named party's capacity to be sued,* or the authority of a party to be sued, the party desiring to raise the issue shall do so by *specific negative averment,* which shall include supporting particulars." (emphasis added)

So? What good does that do?

Well, it means that you can do anything you want to on or with your property as long as you cause no injury or property damage to your neighbors or anyone else. You are not subject to building codes, zoning laws, architectural committee rules, city ordinances, property taxes, homeowners association or condominium rules, regulations or whatever.

All those laws, rules, regulations, ordinances and codes you have always thought applied to you only applied because *you let them apply.* You did not know who you are nor how to rebut the presumption that you are a juristic, corporate being subject to whatever rules and regulations any government body wishes to use to control you.

Get all the editable forms for getting out of all traffic tickets without ever having to go to court, order CD #6 "How to cancel all traffic tickets."

FREEDOM IS *FUN!*

MYTH SEVEN—*We have courts of justice*

Well, we did have courts of law and justice but in 1938 the United States Supreme Court, in a case called *Erie Railroad v. Tompkins*, actually did away with the constitution and the common law and changed our court system from public *law* to public *policy* wherein one is guilty until proven innocent.

In addition, today's courts (judges) are almost universally, hopelessly dishonest and corrupt. Law, justice, fairness or rational thinking have little place in the courts of today and "justice" is largely a thing of the past. Political expediency is more the mark. That is true of the U.S. Supreme Court right on down to the county and city courts.

The following is reprinted by permission from the book *I'm Gonna Bury You!* by Gene Neill, former top criminal defense lawyer.

And there's the corruption.

The incredible corruption. The judges and the cops and the prosecutors and the court reporters and the bailiffs and clerks. They buy and sell cases like they were commodities. A drunk driving case for a couple hundred. A misdemeanor for five. Felonies come a little higher, some of them real high. And a clerk can lose a file or an important pleading or jimmy up the dates on the back of the folder. And the court reporter can change the transcript. Just a word here or a word there can throw a case. Cops can forget the facts or the faces or be sick at home on the last trial date. Little things that'll get a man off. And a prosecutor can accidentally confuse subpoenas so the witnesses aren't there, or neglect to lay the predicate for the introduction of essential fingerprint evidence. Or fail to prove the chain of custody of dope so it can't get into evidence.

Little things.

And no one notices except the judges and cops and lawyers intimately familiar with the case. And if the judge or the prosecutor sees a cop taking a dive on a case he can't say anything because the judge or prosecutor knows that very same cop has seen *him* a hundred times with *his* hand in the cookie jar. So nobody can rat on anybody. And no one wants to anyway.

They just want their piece of the action and the only time there's a hassle is when someone gets cut out of a deal. (Neill 1975, 73).

Disgusting? Of course. *And* that's the way it was in the '70s. It is far, far worse today.

It is the opinion of this writer that what we see in the courts today is God's punishment for a people He blessed beyond anything the world has ever witnessed, because of their complete obedience to His laws, and who then turned their backs on Him and went after more money, movies, TV, newspapers, magazines, sporting events, pornography, the internet and the myriad other things which the devil has sent to pull God's people away from the truth, the Bible, prayer and a dedication to the Lord Jesus Christ.

MYTH BUSTED!

Power tends to corrupt and absolute power corrupts absolutely.

(John Emerich Edward Dalberg)

Former U.S. Supreme Court Chief Justice Warren Burger said, "The attorneys and judges think that they have buried the common law but it rules us from its grave."

U.S. Supreme Court Chief Justice William Rehnquist has said, "Eighty percent of trial lawyers are incompetent!"

That being the case, it should be rather easy to beat an attorney in court. Thank God that it *is* if one takes a few simple steps:

a) NEVER HIRE AN ATTORNEY! Attorneys are officers of the court and are government agents. When you hire one you are hiring an enemy agent and you just lost your cause because, being an officer of the court, his first duty is to that court and the judge and you are third on the list even though you are paying him to work on your behalf. He may appear to be defending your cause but is secretly doing what the judge wishes.

b) When you go into court with an attorney "re-presenting" you, the court (judge) takes *silent judicial notice* that you are incompetent to defend yourself. You are to sit down and shut up and the attorney will do all the talking as your "mouthpiece." You do not have a chance, you poor little incompetent thing, you!

One must remember that not only are attorneys incompetent, they are also, for the most part, lazy because they rely on the judge and public ignorance to cover for them, they write very sloppy and ineffective lawsuits.

BUT HERE'S THE BEST NEWS OF ALL! HALLELUJAH!

You can stay out of court *entirely* if you record an *Affidavit of Denial of Corporate Status* and a *Notice of Copyright* of your STRAW MAN with the county in which you live and be ready to serve them on the plaintiff's attorney and the Clerk of the Court in which you are being sued. *This action will stop any lawsuit,* civil or criminal! See Introduction.

Federal Rules of Civil Procedure, Rule 9(a) states in pertinent part: "When an issue is raised as to the *legal existence of a named party's capacity to be sued, or the authority of a party to be sued,* the party desiring to raise the issue shall do so by *specific negative averment*, which shall include supporting particulars." (emphasis added)

For complete freedom from any and all lawsuits, order CD #7 "How to stop all lawsuits." You will never have to appear in court again!

In addition to CD #7 "How to stop all lawsuits," order CD #9 "How to totally protect your heirs and estate."

That electronic CD contains the complete, editable forms for creating a *Pure Trust* (you can easily write your own, and as many as you need, for complete asset protection).

My people are destroyed for lack of knowledge.

(Hosea 4:6)

FREEDOM IS *FUN!*

MYTH EIGHT—*Banks loan money*

When you go to a bank for a loan for a vehicle, home, investment property or other need or desire and they agree to loan you the amount you need, where do you think the money they are loaning you comes from?

Do you not think that the bank is lending you the money of other depositors? That is what we have all believed for years and what we were taught in the public fool system. But let's take a closer look. . . .

MYTH BUSTED!

When you go to a bank for a loan for any reason, *you* actually create the money you think you are borrowing from the bank! ALL loans are handled the same way whether a mortgage, vehicle loan, credit card account or any other loan. Since they are all handled in the same way, let's just look at mortgages.

This is how it is done: after you have signed the loan application and it has been approved, the bank will ask you to sign a Promissory Note and either a Deed of Trust or a Mortgage depending on the state in which you live.

All paperwork will be made out in the name of your STRAW MAN because the bank, being a fictitious entity, cannot do business with you, a flesh and blood, living, breathing man. But YOU will sign the paperwork, purportedly for your STRAW MAN.

As soon as you affix your signature to the Promissory Note it becomes a negotiable instrument! That means it is the same as cash. **You just created new money!** The bank receives it as cash and accepts it *as a deposit!* Then, in order to make their books balance they create an off-setting credit entry of exactly the same amount out of thin air, new "money" created by a mere computer entry, and *loan your credit to your STRAW MAN.*

It is not *money* which the seller of the property gets, it is *credit* to his account. That credit was produced out of thin air (*monetized*) and the amount of the mortgage has just been added to the economy thus producing more money chasing the same amount of goods in the marketplace and forcing prices higher, causing inflation which fractionalizes your credit and the credit of everyone else.

The banking system is based on fraud, fraud, fraud and is operating a double dip scheme! They're after our *prepaid consideration*.

Read what some of the top insiders have said about the banksters:

Banks lend by creating credit. They create the means of payment out of nothing.

(Ralph M. Hawtrey,
Secretary of the British Treasury)

It is well that the people of the nation do not understand our banking and monetary system for, if they did, I believe there would be a revolution before tomorrow morning.

(Henry Ford)

The regional Federal Reserve Banks are not government agencies but are independent, privately owned and locally controlled corporations.

(*Lewis v. United States*,
680 F.2d 1239 (1982))

*We have in this country one of the most cor-
rupt institutions the world has ever known.
I refer to the Federal Reserve Board. This
evil institution has impoverished the people
of the United States and has practically
bankrupted our government. It has done this
through the corrupt practices of the moneyed
vultures who control it.*

(Congressman Louis T. McFadden [R-PA])

*This [Federal Reserve Act] established the
most gigantic trust on earth. When the
President [Wilson] signs this bill, the invisi-
ble government of the money power will be
legalized . . . the worst legislative crime of
the ages is perpetrated by this banking and
currency bill. From now on, depressions will
be scientifically created.*

(Congressman Charles A.
Lindberg, Sr., 1913)

*When you or I write a check there must be
sufficient funds in our account to cover the
check but when the Federal Reserve writes a
check there is no bank deposit on which that
check is drawn. When the Federal Reserve
writes a check, it is creating money.*

(*Putting it Simply,* Boston Federal
Reserve Bank)

I have never seen more Senators discontent with their jobs . . . I think the major cause is that, deep down in our hearts, we know we have been accomplices in doing something terrible and unforgivable to our wonderful country . . . we know that we have given our children a legacy of bankruptcy. We have defrauded our country to get ourselves re-elected.

(Senator John Danforth, [R-MO])

I believe that banking institutions are more dangerous to our liberties than standing armies. Already they have raised up a monied aristocracy that has set the government at defiance. The issuing [of money] power should be taken away from the banks and restored to the people to whom it properly belongs.

(President Thomas Jefferson)

History records that the money changers have used every form of abuse, intrigue, deceit and violent means possible to maintain their control over governments by controlling money and its issuance.

(President James Madison)

*The individual is handicapped by coming
face to face with a conspiracy so monstrous
he cannot believe it exists.*

(J. Edgar Hoover)

One can easily eliminate one's mortgage
or other debt by essentially demanding that
the so-called "Lender" verify the debt, that
is, prove where the so-called "money"
came from which created the debt. That is
impossible for any bank to do because they
all operate in the fraudulent banking system of which they are a part.

From the book *Modern Money Mechan-
ics*, published by the Federal Reserve Bank:

How the Multiple Expansion Process
Works:

If the process ended here, there would
be no "multiple" expansion, i.e., deposits
and bank reserves would have changed by
the same amount. However, banks are
required to maintain reserves equal to only
a fraction of their deposits. Reserves in
excess of this amount may be used to
increase earning assets—loans and invest-
ments. Unused or excess reserves earn no
interest. Under current regulations, the
reserve requirement against most transac-

tion accounts is 10 percent. Assuming, for simplicity, a uniform 10 percent reserve requirement against all transaction deposits, and further assuming that all banks attempt to remain fully invested, we can now trace the process of expansion in deposits which can take place on the basis of the additional reserves provided by the Federal Reserve System's purchase of U.S. government securities.

The expansion process may or may not begin with Bank A, depending on what the dealer does with the money received from the sale of securities. If the dealer immediately writes checks for $10,000 and all of them are deposited in other banks, Bank A loses both deposits and reserves and shows no net change as a result of the System's open market purchase. However, other banks have received them. Most likely, a part of the initial deposit will remain with Bank A, and a part will be shifted to other banks as the dealer's checks clear.

It does not really matter where this money is at any given time. The important fact is that these deposits do not disappear. They are in some deposit accounts at all times. All banks together have $10,000 of deposits and reserves **that they did not have before**. However, they are not required to keep

$10,000 of reserves against the $10,000 of deposits. All they need to retain, under a 10 percent reserve requirement, is $1,000. The remaining $9,000 is "excess reserves." This amount can be loaned or invested.

If business is active, the banks with excess reserves probably will have opportunities to loan the $9,000. Of course, they do not really pay out loans from the money they receive as deposits. If they did this, no additional money would be created. What they do when they make loans is to **accept promissory notes in exchange for credits to the borrowers' transaction accounts**. Loans (assets) and deposits (liabilities) both rise by $9,000. Reserves are unchanged by the loan transactions. But the deposit credits constitute **new additions to the total deposits of the banking system**. (emphasis added)

There you see it admitted in their own publication! *Your* Promissory Note allowed the so-called "Lender" to *create new money out of thin air* and charge you interest on such created money which is called usury.

It costs next to nothing for the "Lender" to make you that mortgage loan or any other loan. In fact, read your Promissory

Note or Deed of Trust or Mortgage carefully and you will find that "Lender" and "Borrower" are in quotation marks.

The following is from the Purdue University online writing lab:

Quotation Marks for Words—Use quotation marks to indicate words used ironically, with reservations, or in some unusual way.

Quotation marks suggest that the word is being used in an unusual way and that **something else is really meant**. (emphasis added)

http://owl.english.purdue.edu/index.htm

This gives us an idea of the subtlety of the deception of the banksters, sneaking in words in quotes that actually mean something else. BEWARE THE BANKSTERS!!!

In other words, "Lender" really means "we are just calling them the lender" and "Borrower" really means "we are just calling them the borrower." They are both actually *something else*.

Nice work if you can get it, right? The banksters get away with loaning us back our own credit and tricking us into repaying it to them with interest. No wonder the largest buildings in every city are the bank buildings! What a sweet racket!

Get your mortgage debt eliminated and donate the money saved to the Lord's work! That's what I and a great many others have done. Purchase electronic CD #8 "How to eliminate your mortgage."

FREEDOM IS *FUN!*

MYTH NINE—*You should have a will*

When people consider how they wish to divide up their estate upon their demise, they usually consult an attorney. The attorney will almost always advise them to draw up a will which will lay out all their assets and dictate who is to receive how much of the estate. There are even many churches and at least one entire denomination who offer to have member attorneys draw up wills free for their various members!

Alternatively, the attorney will suggest forming a statutory trust, either a living trust, revocable trust or irrevocable trust with a "pour over will" which will contain everything not already in the trust and designate it to be included in the trust on the demise of the settlor of the trust. A statutory trust will typically be *recorded with the county of domicile* of the settlor. The settlor(s) is/are the parties putting the property (assets) into the trust.

MYTH BUSTED!

A will or statutory trust, by whatever name, is the slickest, easiest way for dishonest attorneys and judges to steal the assets of an estate. Untold *trillions of dollars* have been stolen in this manner.

My great-grandfather invented the roller skate in the mid 1800s and became a millionaire in the days when a million dollars was an *immense* amount of money and there were no income taxes!

He had a will which had been drawn up by his attorney. All wills must go to, and hopefully *through*, the probate court. Who sits in charge of the probate court but an attorney in a black robe called a judge. The judge in my great-grandfather's probate case conspired with his attorney to steal his entire estate and left his estate bankrupt with $30,000 of debt.

Slick as can be! There was no recourse because it was done by "the court." If you have a will, or statutory trust, you can expect a large portion, if not all, of your estate to "disappear" in probate and there will be nothing you or your heirs can do about it.

What is one to do then? Well there is an excellent solution in having the settlor(s), whoever is putting property into the trust, create a *pure* trust, otherwise called a common law trust or Massachusetts trust (because it is a favorite with the Kennedys and other super wealthy folk?). That is a private contract trust created under our constitutionally protected *unlimited right to contract.* It is not recorded or filed with any government body so no judge or attorney can wriggle their way in to steal the assets.

Upon the demise of the settlor, the assets go directly and immediately into the hands of the designated beneficiaries. No probate, no stealing, no holdup. There is immediate distribution to the beneficiaries unless it is decided by the trustee of the trust to hold the assets and distribute any income derived from those assets to the beneficiaries. Simple, inexpensive, effective and safe.

EXCELLENT ASSET PROTECTION

When Ted Kennedy drove his car off the bridge at Chappaquiddick Island resulting in the drowning death of Mary Jo Kopeckni, the Kopeckni family consulted an attorney about filing a wrongful death lawsuit against the Massachusetts senator. The attorney's investigation revealed that Senator Kennedy had no attachable income and no property, therefore he was "uncollectible" and there was no point wasting time and money on a lawsuit.

It was reported that Senator Kennedy was the manager of over 150 trusts. He had each of his properties, vehicles, airplanes, boats, etc. in a separate trust. He did not own the vehicle in which Ms. Kopeckni was drowned. It belonged to a trust so all the Kopeckni family could possibly get was one water-soaked Oldsmobile and a small insurance policy on it.

THAT is excellent asset protection!

BEWARE! **There are a great many attorneys who will tell you imaginary war stories about how the pure trusts have gotten people into deep trouble and to stay away from them at all costs. Attorneys even have Web sites which**

post a great deal of unsupported, unverified propaganda trying to scare folks into going to them for statutory trusts so that they will be able to steal the assets when they go to probate.

Probate court is a monstrous racket run by attorneys and attorneys in black robes called judges. I repeat, untold *trillions* of dollars have been stolen in probate courts over the years and it seems to get worse every year.

Be sure and order electronic CD #9 "How to totally protect your heirs and estate." It contains all the editable forms needed to write your own pure trusts for complete asset protection.

Governments, judges and attorneys *hate* pure trusts because they are precluded from stealing the assets of the people. Isn't that sad?

FREEDOM, THOUGH, IS CERTAINLY *FUN!*

MYTH TEN—*You should incorporate your business*

When people start a new business of any kind they usually go to an attorney and an accountant who will both advise them to incorporate their business in order to limit their liability should anything go wrong, accidents occur, suits for damages of any kind be filed, etc.

They will tell clients that to do so will limit clients' liability to one extent or another. Nothing could be further from the truth. It is a governmental TRAP!

MYTH BUSTED!

, Incorporating a business is a *trap* set for us by government and we must remember that lawyers and accountants are government agents who want to do everything possible to bring us under government control with the hopes of getting future fees from us.

Remember what you learned about the STRAW MAN in the introduction to this book. Governments, being corporate municipal *fictions,* can only deal with other *fictions,* hence their need to incorporate your business in order to bring you under their control.

Only an attorney can represent a corporate entity. You cannot represent any corporation in court so you *must* hire an attorney and, when you do, you are hiring an "officer of the court," really an enemy agent who will sell you and your interests down the river in a heartbeat.

WHAT IS THE SOLUTION?

The solution is simple. NEVER INCORPORATE YOUR BUSINESS! Run the business under *your own name* if you possibly can or as a pure trust. What will that do for you? It will eliminate the need for insurance of any kind, workmen's compensation, and make you *IMMUNE from any and all lawsuits!*

Purchase CD #10 "How to avoid the incorporation trap" for a complete explanation of the various ways to run a business unincorporated and free from the laws, rules, regulations, ordinances, etc. which the government has thought up to entrap and enslave us.

FREEDOM IS BOTH *FUN* AND *PROFITABLE!*

UNIFORM COMMERCIAL CODE (UCC) EXPLAINED

If you were to ask 500 people, including attorneys, accountants and others of their ilk, "What can you tell me about the UCC?" you would get about 500 blank stares. Some might profess to have heard of it, but no one would be able to explain it to you. Yet the astounding fact is that *the UCC rules and regulates our lives every moment of every day!*

Several years ago someone told me, "You will never win in court, or understand what is really going on around you, until you understand the Uniform Commercial Code." So I determined to understand it and went to our public library where I found that *the UCC took up about nine feet of shelf space!*

It seemed a daunting if not impossible task to do the research which would lead to an understanding of the UCC so I waited for others more competent than I to understand it.

The first was Howard Griswold of Delaware, a very experienced researcher, who discovered UCC 1–207 which established one's self as being under common law right as follows (Sec. 1-207 has been replaced by Sec 1–308 in the latest version of the UCC), hence:

> *My use of the statement "Without preju-*
> *dice UCC 1–308" below my signature on this*
> *document indicates that I have exercised the*
> *remedy provided for me in the Uniform Com-*
> *mercial Code in Article 1, Sec. 308 whereby I*
> *might reserve my common law right not to be*
> *found or compelled to perform under any*
> *contract, commercial agreement or bank-*
> *ruptcy that I did not enter into knowingly,*
> *voluntarily and intentionally. And further-*
> *more, that reservation notifies all adminis-*
> *trative agencies of government that I do not,*
> *and will not, accept the liability associated*
> *with the compelled benefit of any unrevealed*
> *contract, commercial agreement or bank-*
> *ruptcy, (per Howard Griswold).*

Pretty heady stuff! Any contract you autograph, placing "Without prejudice UCC 1–308" or even just "Without Preju-dice" either above or below your auto-graph, is null and void just as though it had never happened. This applies to a traffic ticket or any other "contract" you would rather not participate in but are being coerced to do so. Just write "Without Prejudice" in the signature box of the traffic ticket and hand it back to the officer.

Another handy tool available under the UCC is called a UCC Financing Statement. It is a document filed with the Secretary of State in most states or Department of Licensing in Washington state.

When you file one against your STRAW MAN as debtor with yourself as Secured Party Creditor posting the title to your home, automobiles and other personal property as collateral, you have first place lien against anyone wishing to take your property for any reason. That means that, in order to take your property, they must first pay you full appraised value of it.

Of course it will seldom come to that since you will stop forward action of the court by the service of your Affidavit of Denial of Corporate Status and Notice of Copyright of your STRAW MAN with the Clerk of Court, opposing attorney and any other authority involved.

Your Notice of Copyright is actually a self-effectuating contract which carries with it a $100,000 penalty for *each* unauthorized use of your copyrighted property in Commerce without your express written permission signed in red ink! When you send an invoice to an attorney, bureaucrat, mortgage company, title company or whatever, you will notice things get very quiet.

That is because they must pay the invoice in full within twenty days or you send them a Notice of Fault giving them the Biblical "notice and grace" of three further days in which to pay it or make suitable arrangements to do so.

If they do not respond to the notice of fault, how can they, they agreed to it via the Notice of Copyright, you send them a Notice of Default. When they ignore that, you then file a UCC Financing Statement against each party who has used your copyrighted property in Commerce without your permission and that will show up on their credit report!

This is serious business. You can take their property under strict foreclosure or nonjudicial foreclosure and auction off whatever they may own up to the amount of the debt they owe you. This is all made possible with the latest revision in UCC Section 9, June 1, 2001, which was designed to allow the banksters to steal our property from us without having to go to court. We have been able to reverse it on them because, as we said above, hardly anyone knows about the UCC or how to use it.

All the necessary forms listed in this book and help in using them are available on editable electronic CDs from The Boaz Trust.

Note: All net proceeds from the sale of my CDs will go toward funding ministries of the Lord Jesus Christ. NONE, of course, will go to 501(c)(3) State agencies!

A workman is worthy of his hire.
(Jesus Christ, quoted in Matthew 10:10)

I hope that this work has been eye-opening and interesting for you, gentle reader, and wish to remind you that

FREEDOM IS CERTAINLY *FUN!*

APPENDIX

True, total and complete freedom comes only from God through His Son Jesus Christ of Nazareth. "It is the Lord who sets the prisoners free" (Psalms 146:7). Jesus Himself tells us:

"You shall know the truth and the truth shall set you free" (John 8:32). "If the Son sets you free, you shall be free indeed" (John 8:36).

Yes, pilgrim, there is no freedom on this earth like the freedom one knows with Christ Jesus. Daniel Webster said, "Education without the Bible is useless." If one wants true and lasting freedom, one must study the Bible and follow its instructions.

My late friend, Harold Hill, author of *How to Live Like A King's Kid*, called the Bible "The Manufacturer's Handbook." And that it is. When something goes wrong in our lives, the solution to the problem can be found in the Bible. The words of an old favorite hymn express it well: "Oh what peace we often forfeit, Oh what needless pain we bear, all because we do not carry everything to God in prayer."

I was privileged to be engaged in prison ministry for about fifteen years, taking the Bible and the glorious gospel (good news) of Jesus into prisons in many parts of this country. I have personally witnessed miracles among inmates—lives turned from sheer hatred to abounding love, hundreds of healings and salvations, miraculous releases from prison with no explanation but the supernatural working of the Holy Spirit of God as He got through to the men.

God is no respecter of persons. What He has done for millions of others He will do for you if you surrender your heart to Him and *walk* in His way, not just *talk* in His way. God is after every one of us to get us to walk ever closer with Him so He can give us the peace, love and blessings which He has waiting for every believer.

A journey of a thousand miles begins with the first step. The first step in our spiritual journey is our acceptance of Jesus Christ as our Lord and Savior. A simple prayer from the heart will do it. Just something like this—*Lord Jesus, I'm not really sure you are out there, but, if you are out there somewhere, I cry out to you to forgive my sins completely, come into my heart and be the ruler of my life. I am tired of living my own way and need you to take over and run things for me. I will follow whatever you tell me to do. Thank you for forgiving my sins and taking over the control of my life. In Your Wonderful Name I pray. AMEN!*

If you prayed that prayer from your heart for the first time, the Bible says that all heaven is rejoicing! Be sure to tell some-one! Don't think your trials are over though. The Bible tells us "Many are the trials of the righteous but the Lord delivers him out of them all! (Psalms 34:17–19). GOD BLESS YOU!

TRUE FREEDOM IS *FUN!*

Note: It is my desire to share the knowledge gained over the past twenty years with as many people as possible.
Please remember that scientific research has shown that, once we leave formal edu-cation, it takes a repetition of **7 times** in order to get new knowledge anchored in our psyche. This book is an easy read of less than 2 hours so you can master the basic concepts in less than a week depending on

your desire to achieve freedom and the amount of time you devote to the study.

The knowledge presented here is really earth-shaking and a definite departure from the things we were taught in the government run 'public fool system'! Be patient, give yourself some time to acclimatize yourself to a completely new way of looking at things. You will find it will be well worth it.

Please don't be shy about sharing this book and its knowledge with others by downloading it from *www.elimadebts.com* and emailing it to the folks in your address book. It is not copyrighted and may be distributed as far and wide as you may wish. It is a very important educational tool.

For further information you may want to visit *www.elimadebts.com* where you can read amazing facts and details which may well make you weep at having been given so much misleading, untrue and deceptive information in the course of your formal education. I felt that way myself when I was first exposed to this knowledge!

Although my electronic CDs are completely self explanatory and do-it-yourself enabled, many people feel squeamish about doing it themselves, at least at first, and are willing to pay to have someone do it for them. If you have the capability of running an orderly office and the equipment with which to service customers, computer, printer, file cabinets, office space (if even in a home) and a clear grasp of the various MYTHS in my book, you may wish to become a Consultant. If so, please visit *www.elimadebts.com* and click on the Consultant Agreement tab.

Best wishes and may God richly bless, guide and sustain you as you learn about your course to true freedom.

I, Bob Plimpton, can tell you from personal experience that

FREEDOM IS *FUN!*

"You were BORN FREE, now you can LIVE FREE!

The astounding **NEW** set of 10 electronic CDs from The Boaz Trust.

(7) CD #1 How to avoid the birth certificate trap

(8) CD #2 How to avoid the social security trap

(9) CD #3 How to avoid the marriage license trap

(1) CD #4 How to deal with debt collectors and win

(2) CD #5 How to legally stop paying income taxes

(3) CD #6 How to cancel all traffic tickets

(10) CD #7 How to stop all lawsuits

(6) CD #8 How to eliminate your mortgage

(4) CD #9 How to totally protect your heirs and estate

(5) CD #10 How to avoid the incorporation trap

It's so simple—you just edit the forms to your name(s) and mail them! Complete instructions are on every electronic CD.

Each electronic CD is an incredible bargain at only $69.99! OR The entire set of 10 electronic CDs for only $599.00.

One visit to a lawyer could cost you many times that amount!

And no lawyer knows all the secrets contained on these CDs.

Order the electronic CDs by visiting *www.elimadebts.com* and clicking the Freedom Book tab. OR designate the electronic CDs you wish to purchase and send check or money order to:

The Boaz Trust
4371 Northlake Blvd., #303
Palm Beach Gardens, FL 33410

GUARANTEE: If for any reason at any time, you feel disappointed in any way with the knowledge you will gain from these electronic CDs, simply visit me at www.elimadebts.com/support.aspx and you will receive a full refund. May God richly bless, guide and sustain you in your new found FREEDOM!

Bob Plimpton